To

From

From the publishers

Hello! We hope you have you enjoyed this title. A review would be greatly appreciated if you could spare a moment. We have put a lot of effort into creating this book, but if you are not completely satisfied, then please email mary-ann@maryannbooks.com and we will do our best to get it sorted.

If this book is misprinted, email us with the misprint and we will send another!

My drawing of us!

1

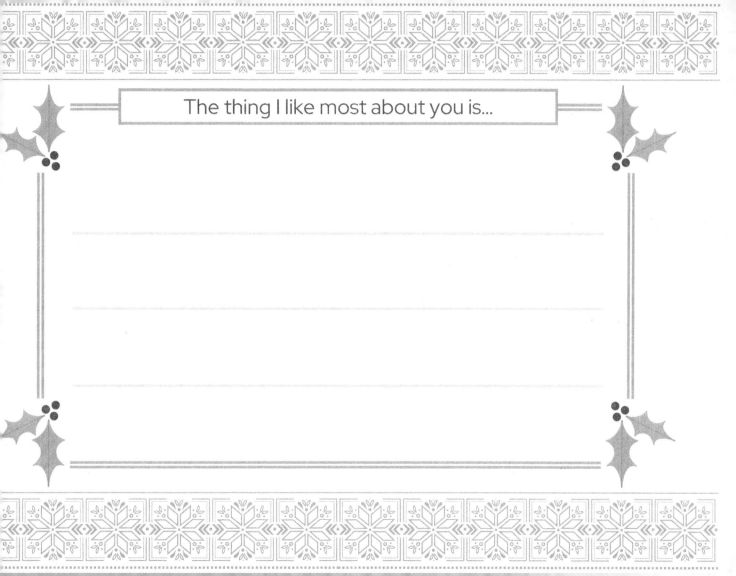

The thing I like most about you is...

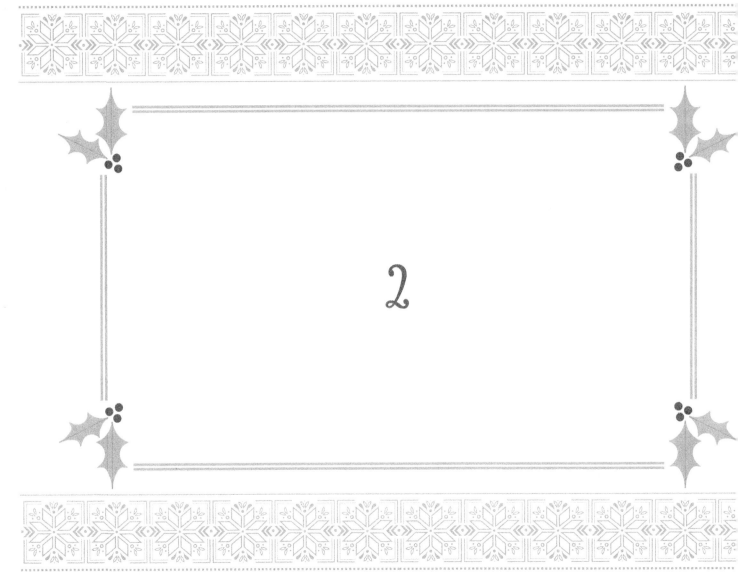

You make me laugh the most when...

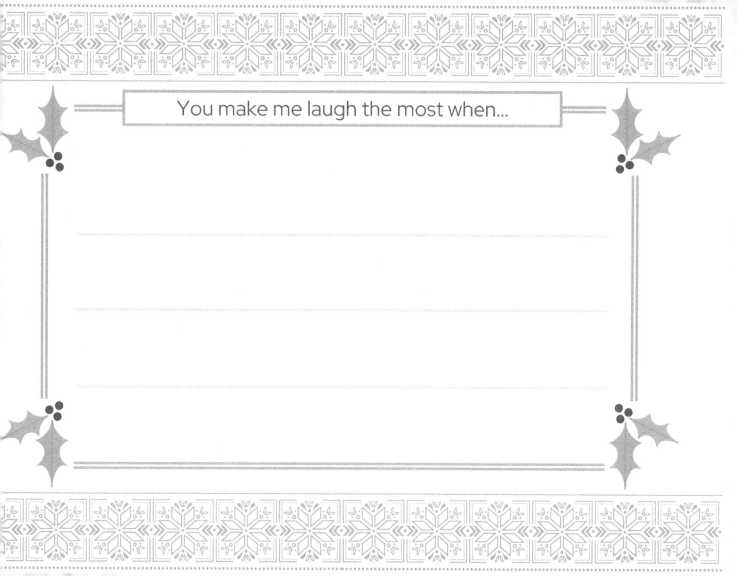

3

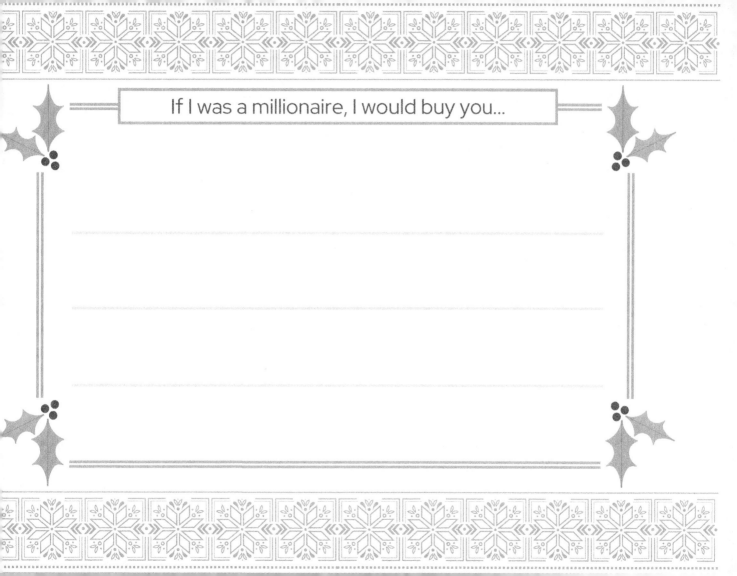

If I was a millionaire, I would buy you...

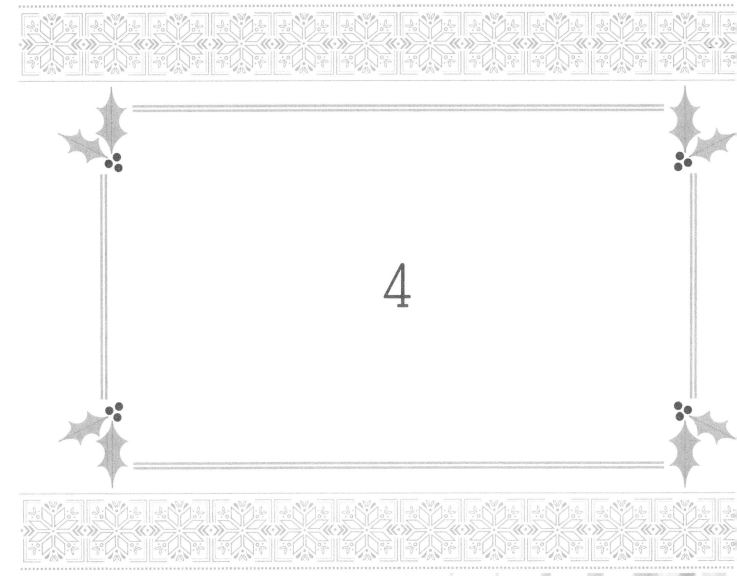

4

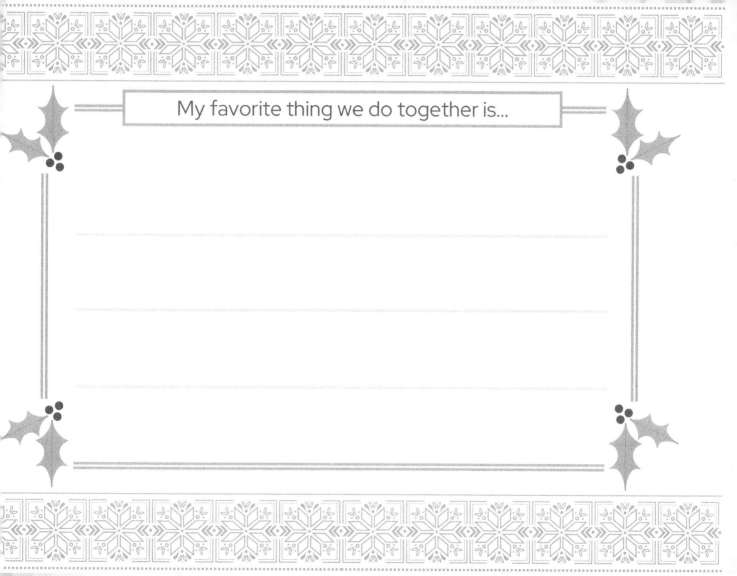

My favorite thing we do together is...

5

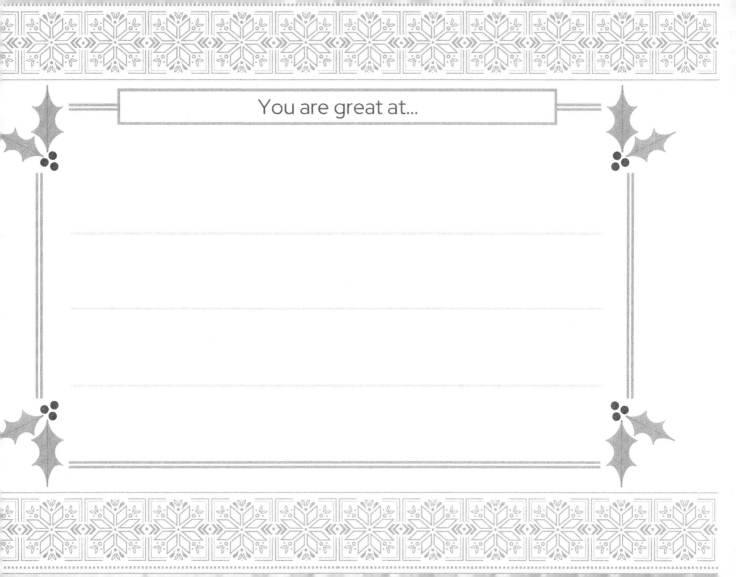

You are great at...

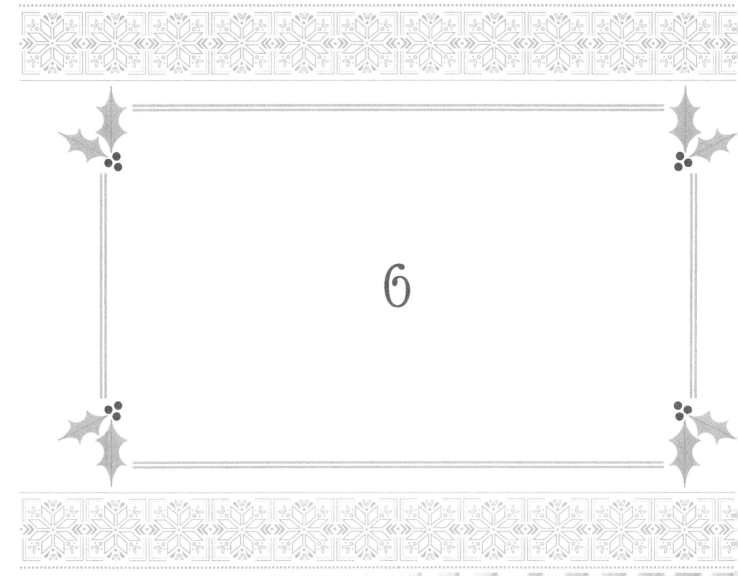

6

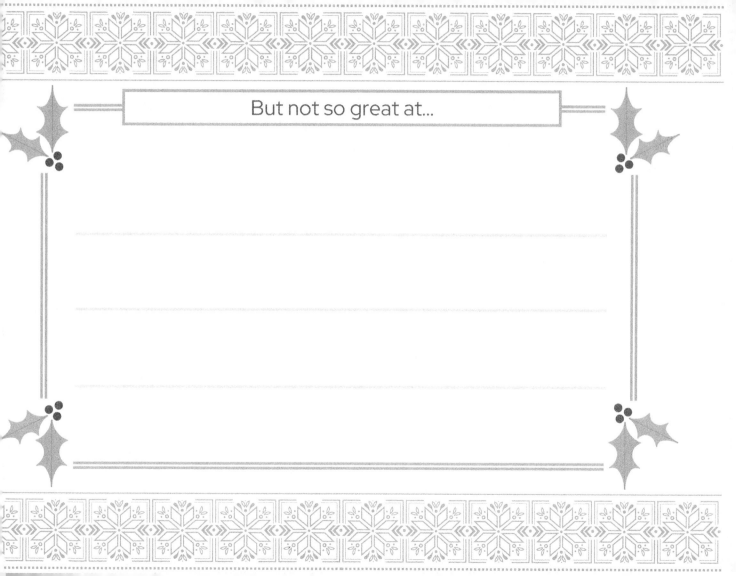

But not so great at...

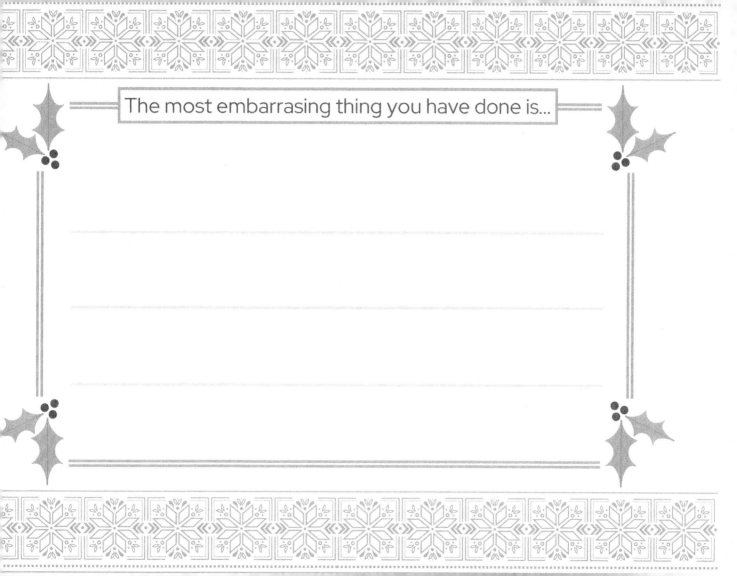

The most embarrasing thing you have done is...

If you had a superpower, it would be...

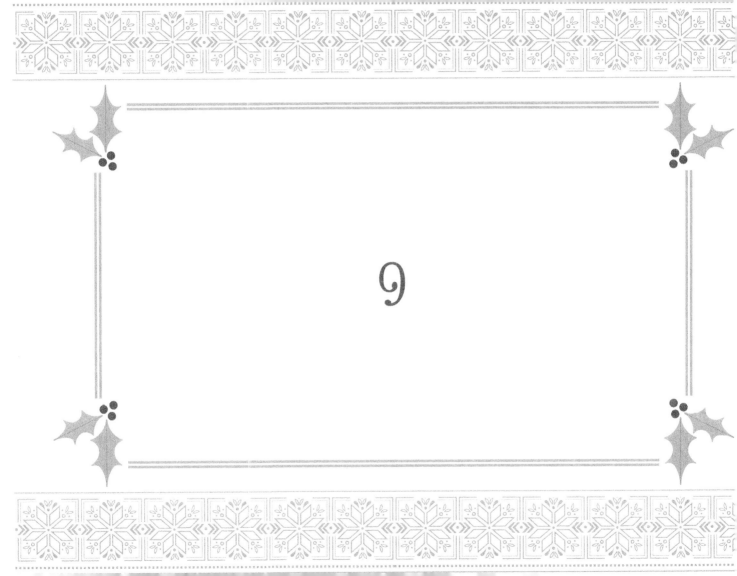

People that know you would say you are...

10

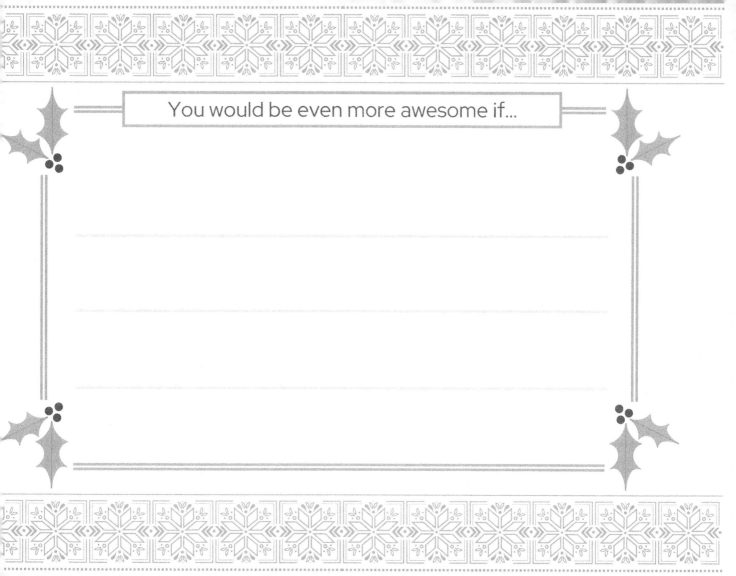

You would be even more awesome if...

11

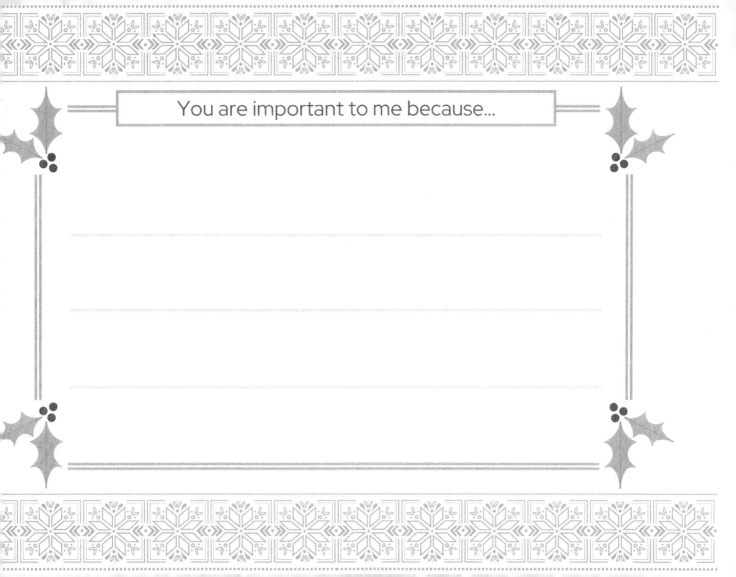

You are important to me because...

12

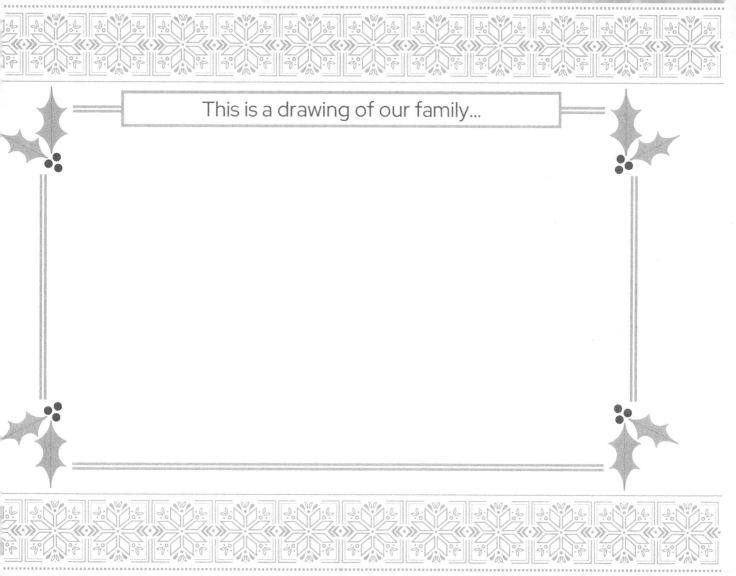

This is a drawing of our family...

13

One thing you taught me was...

14

Your favorite food is...

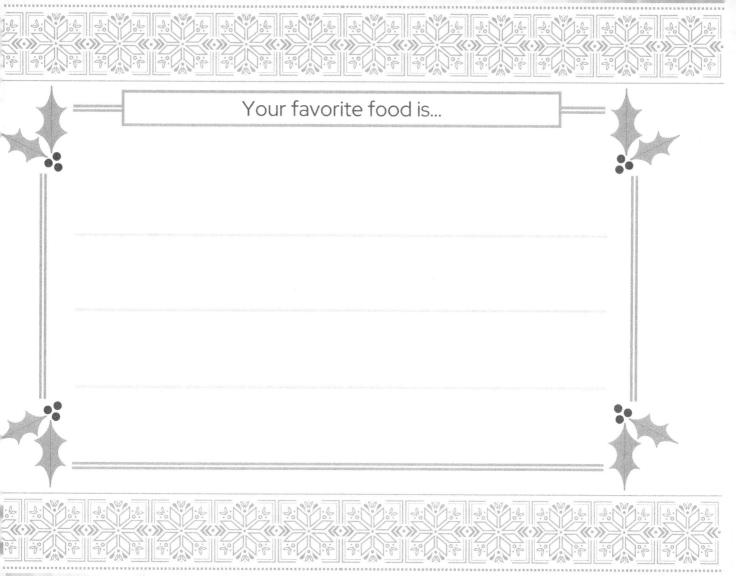

15

My favorite memory of us is...

16

My favorite trip together so far is...

17

This Christmas, we should...

18

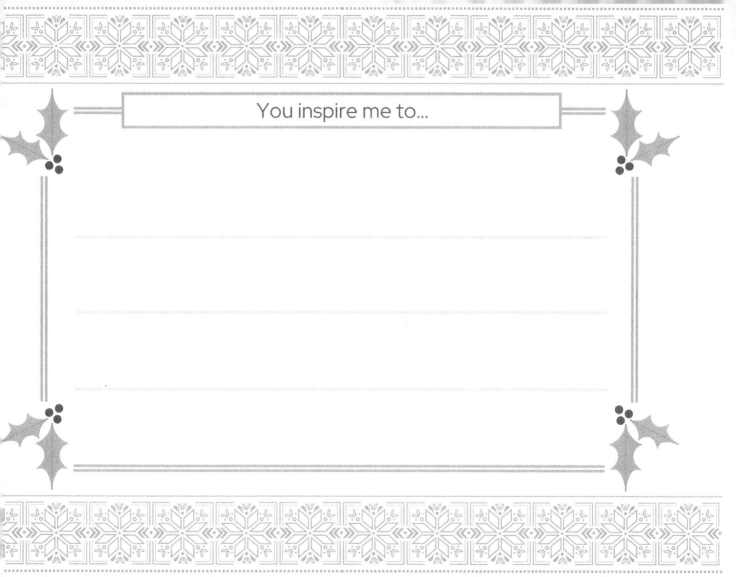

You inspire me to...

19

I wish I was as good as you at...

20

When I am an adult, I will be...

21

You always say...

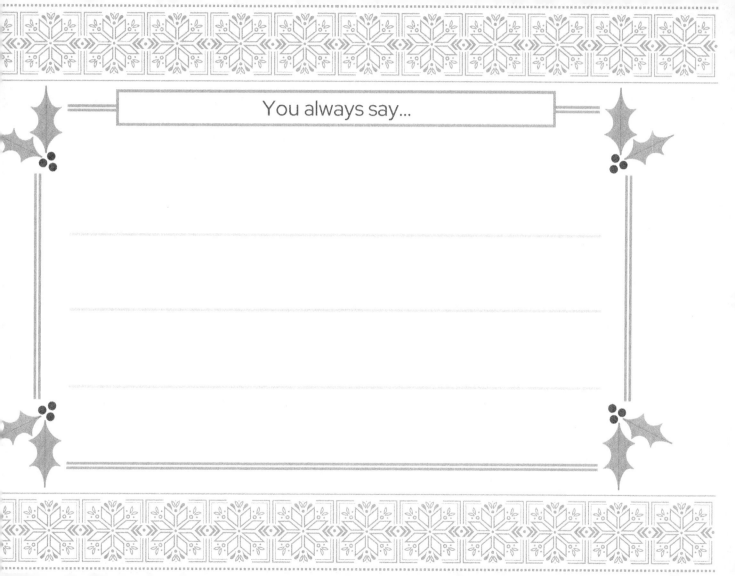

22

You love to tell stories about...

23

Your ideal Christmas present is...

24

Something special in the future I would like to do with you is...

Here's a collection
of photos I have
put together!

Made in the USA
Monee, IL
09 December 2024

73034735R00037